He's Able!

Jimi

He is for You!

Shurmi

GRANNY PAID FOR OUR DIVORCE

JIMMIE AND SHERRI BRATCHER

Granny Paid for Our Divorce
By Jimmie and Sherri Bratcher

ISBN 978-0-692-64804-9

Find out more about Jimmie and Sherri's ministry at
www.jimmiebratcher.com

Gungor Publishing

For information, address inquiries to: info@laughyourway.com
www.markgungor.com

Design by Debbie Bishop

Some vector graphics: Designed by Freepik
and by Designerhrenov / Freepik, Mary1507 / Freepik and Kjpargeter / Freepik

Printed in China

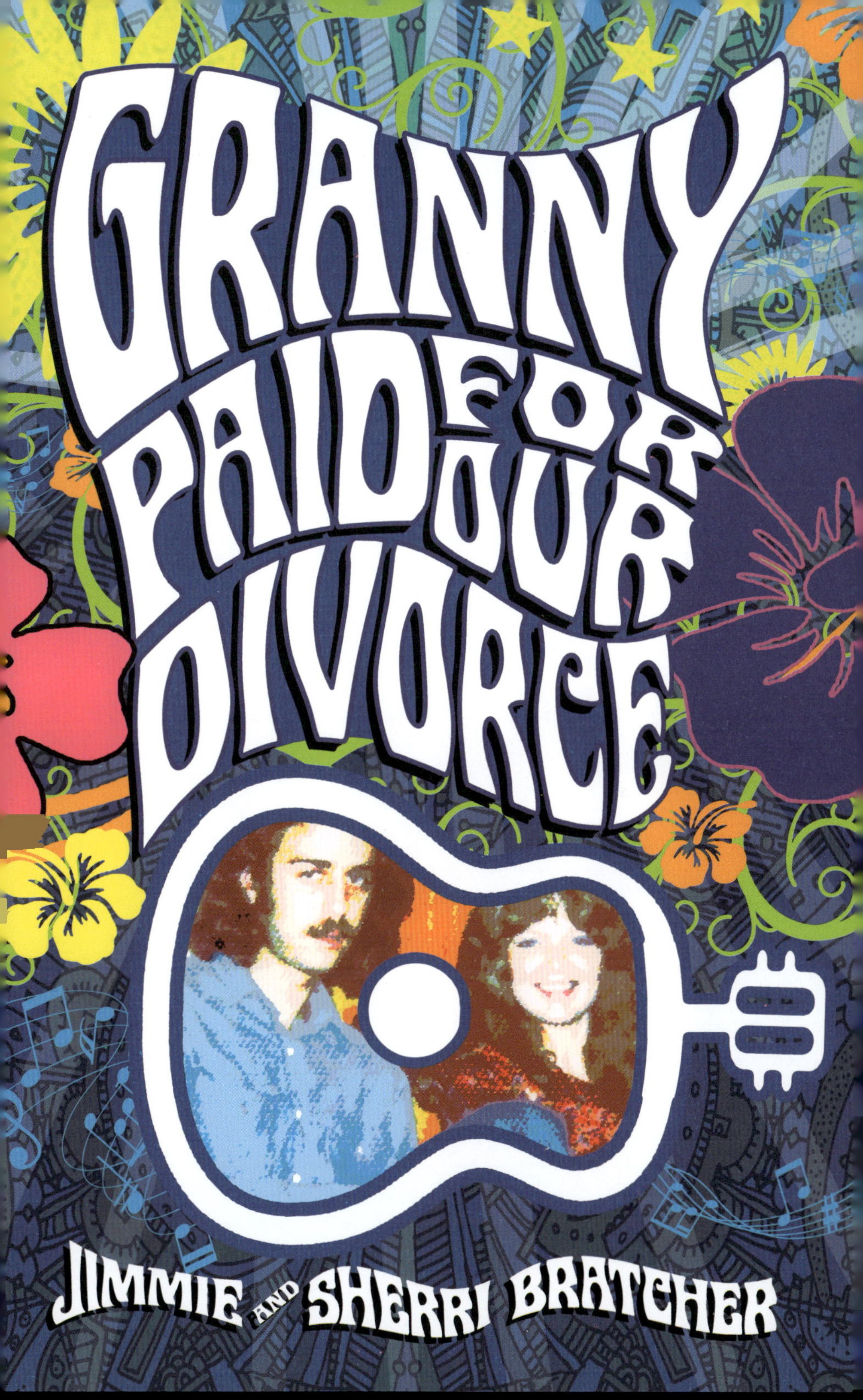
GRANNY PAID FOR OUR DIVORCE
JIMMIE AND SHERRI BRATCHER

To the one that could save us from ourselves.

Thank you, Jesus…

"God rewrote the text of my life

when I opened the book of my heart to his eyes."

2 Samuel 22:25 (MSG)

Contents

Introduction

I, Jimmie, love happy endings! If I go to a movie and it doesn't have a happy ending, I will go to the ticket counter and ask for a refund. I am not going to pay for a movie with a sad ending. Someone else might, but not me. Right now, all of us are working, building toward our own happy ending. It's being written, moment by moment, breath by breath, decision by decision. The great thing about the story is that it's yours. You get to choose how the story goes and how it ends. So why not choose a happy ending?

Our desire in writing our story is that you may know that it doesn't matter where you start. Our hope in writing our story is that something that we say will inspire you; that something in our story will give you the faith and hope to face the chaos and confusion in your own life, make wise choices and start rewriting your own story.

These pages contain some of our family's most painful moments in life. To be honest, it was really hard to write this book because we had to again relive the pain and bad decisions that nearly cost us our family. But, we got to relive the victories.

We are so proud of our family; we love our family more than anything else on this earth. They have taught us what really matters and taught us how to laugh. We have walked through all of our greatest victories together, and that is what made all of those victories possible. This book is about our family and the crazy path we took to where we are. Yes, Granny did pay for our divorce, but that is only part of the story.

Peace,

Jimmie & Sherri

Jimmie & Sherri

CHAPTER ONE

The Trailer Queen and the Wannabe Rockstar

I was born and raised in Excelsior Springs, Missouri, and it was a happening town; it was a spa town. People came there for many reasons, but most of them came for the water—mineral water. Excelsior Springs has more different types of mineral water than any other place in the world. People came by the tens of thousands for mineral water treatments and to go to the world-renowned Elms Hotel, The Ball Clinic, The Hall of Waters, Excelsior Springs Golf Course, many other resorts and several church camps.

As long as I can remember, my maternal and paternal grandparents were in my life.

My paternal grandparents lived in Orrick, Missouri, not far from Excelsior Springs. Through the years, we lived with both sets of my grandparents at different times. We also lived with my Aunt Lollitta and Uncle George (on my Dad's side). They had three children who were all a few years older than me, but they always watched out for and took care of my brother Mark and me. They lived on a farm so it made life really interesting and fun.

One Sunday morning we were up getting ready to go to church. My folks were both working, so Aunt Lollitta got me completely ready and then went to get herself ready. By the time she came back, I had climbed into her cold, dusty fireplace with my pretty little dress on, and well, you know what ashes do! She

Elmer (Sonny) & Evelyn Fletcher

didn't get mad, she just picked me up and started over. I have such fond memories of time spent with them.

Growing up, my family moved many times. My dad had a hard time finding work, so we moved around a lot. While I was really young, during the time we lived in Joplin, Missouri, good news came one day that my dad found a job driving a truck in Kansas City. Because it was closer, we moved back to Excelsior Springs. My folks bought a house where my dad Elmer Jr., my mom Evelyn, my older brother Mark and I lived. We were so proud of our new house. It was brand new, in a great neighborhood and near Golf Hill.

My brother and I were very close! He watched out for me always and I looked out for him. He taught me how to drive! He was my best friend growing up and still is today.

I remember one time my grandparents pulled up at our house with some abandoned puppies that my grandfather found while working on a sight for The Missouri Power and Light Company. He let us pick which one we wanted and I named him Bingo. Bingo was a Shepherd/Lab mix, long black hair with white on his chest. He was beautiful and was protective of me. I loved that part of my life, but soon we had to move out of our house into a 10x30 two bedroom trailer.

While I have some fond memories of my childhood, there always seemed to be a lot of conflict, anger, frustration, and poverty in our house. I never felt safe there, every part of my life was chaotic. Four people living in a 10x30 two-bedroom trailer is hard enough, but then when you add in the irrational, sometimes explosive, demands of my mother, it pushed everything over the top. I never knew what to expect whenever I would come home and open the door. I wouldn't know what I was walking into. Would she be happy or would she get angry? Then to add to the stress, we barely made ends meet. That's just a nice way to say that we were poor. We had food most of the time, even if it was only tomato soup or grilled cheese sandwiches. I always felt that I needed to fix everything. If my mom was sad I would try to find a way to make it better. I felt the same way toward my dad, grandmother, grandfather and brother! After a while, I didn't want to take care of anyone anymore. I needed someone to take care of me, to love and protect me.

I share this next part only to help people who have broken relationships with their loved ones. I was very close to my dad, he always made me laugh, and I felt safe with him. I always felt loved and accepted by him. I loved my mother dearly, but we did not have a healthy relationship. I could talk to my dad about anything when he was present but I couldn't talk to my mom about anything. My mom always made me feel like I was never good enough, like I was always wrong, like I was unimportant. In some ways it seemed she felt I was a threat to her or somehow in competition with her. It was crazy, but that's the way it was. She was always screaming at me, and as I got older, the screaming turned into hitting, pushing and shoving. It wasn't until late in her life that she was able to really be the mom I always knew she wanted to be.

Talking to my brother Mark over the years, he said that he recognized the issues Mom had toward me and how she treated me like a rival and not her daughter. He said that she would try to do the same to him, but he would just leave. I didn't have that option.

I didn't really identify this conflict with my

mom till much later in life. I don't know if I was in denial, or if it was because I didn't want to shame her, even though it caused me great pain.

When I was eight years old, my parents divorced and my dad moved to Kansas City. I was devastated. I felt very lost in all of it! Soon after they split up we had to sell our house. I didn't want to move from there because it was the only time we were not living with anyone else. When we were living in that house, I felt like we were a real family.

When my parents divorced I never could grasp what that would truly mean. I remember asking my grandparents and my mom, "Does this mean he isn't my dad anymore? Does this mean I won't see him again? Does this mean he doesn't love me or want me anymore?" I was so heartbroken, hurt, angry and alone.

Since we had nowhere to go, my grandparents bought a trailer and put it on a lot next to their house and we moved in there. But soon after we moved to the trailer, my brother came home and announced he, too, was moving to Kansas City with my dad. I was too young to make that choice, so I felt completely abandoned, alone and afraid. I always felt loved by my dad; he was a safe place for me and I felt loved and safe with my brother, too. It was very scary for me when they both left. No one noticed I felt scared and lonely. I was just left to myself.

I hope what I am saying will help those of you reading this to learn to be a safe place for your kids. Let them talk to you about everything and don't freak out, (hippy term). They are gonna find some answer somewhere, and it should be led by you. It's proven knowledge that anything left to itself only gets worse and decays.

A few years after the divorce, I had a very inappropriate encounter with a family member that rocked my world. It was with someone whom I had always trusted, but now that trust was violated and all I felt was fear and anxiety. From that moment on I had to protect myself and not allow myself to ever be anywhere alone with that person. The most devastating thing about this event was that no one noticed. No one noticed that I didn't want to go with this family member anymore—no one saw the warning signs of abuse. Again, no one noticed how scared, lonely and angry I was. I was left to myself with no one I could talk to. I felt invisible. Besides those horrible emotions, I knew that no one would believe me.

So I hid myself behind a wall of anger. When I hit my teens, that's when I really began to be rebellious against everything. All the anger of feeling alone and abandoned and uncared for caused me to make some personal constitutions! You know, some deep decisions—some good and some not so good.

Even though my parents had divorced, they would still get back together then separate, then get back together and separate again. They did this several times. I could not stand to be at home. I dreaded being there because it was always full of strife! One day, out of nowhere, while I was in the kitchen fixing a sandwich, my mom came in and began to scream at me and call me names. I had no idea what caused her attack. I can't remember why, but then she called me a bitch and threw orange juice in my face. At that point, I was done.

In the eighth grade, I had to find some relief, so I just left. I couldn't take the chaos, the fear, the loneliness. I had to protect myself because no one else would. So, I stayed with friends at their parents' house and searched for some way to stop the pain. Soon, I started taking diet pills; I felt like I had to escape. But before long I began doing many more types of drugs: pot, acid, MDA, THC, PCP. But my drugs of choice were speed or Quaaludes. Completely opposite feelings—one up, one down. Basically, I did whatever I could get my hands on.

It was a weird time for everyone in the late '60s, very unsettling. Rock and roll, riots, sex and free love (by the way, nothing's for free, especially not love), the Vietnam War, President John F. Kennedy was killed, then Dr. Martin Luther King, then Robert F. Kennedy as well. Lots of craziness and chaos everywhere. In the midst of all this, my mom and dad were split up again, because my grandfather had forced my dad to leave. My brother Mark got drafted into the Army and had to go fight in Vietnam. I was so afraid for him, so I escaped more and more into a life of chaos.

Chaos and confusion best described my life. I had no boundaries and I had to figure out everything on my own.

While I was away from home, my grandfather became very ill. This forced me to go back and face my family…and when I did, it was not good. I was only about 16 when he became ill. As I mentioned earlier, I had made some personal constitutions; one of them was I didn't want to take care of my family anymore. I was angry because I didn't feel like they had ever taken care of me. So, I left the hospital that night, went downtown, and looking down Thompson Avenue, I screamed out loud, "AS OF TODAY I DON'T GIVE A DAMN!"

But the truth, is I wanted love, acceptance, someone to care for me like I cared for them. So I went "lookin' for love in all the wrong places." You know that song...

I graduated from high school but didn't even go to the ceremony. I knew that none of my family would even care enough to show up. I knew no one would support me, so the school just mailed my diploma to me. The main reason I even made it through school and graduated was because of a wonderful teacher who showed great interest in me: Dorothea McCullough. She was a gem.

In my senior year I also got to go to Wright's Business School in Kansas City and I learned business skills. But what I believed about myself didn't allow me to stay at any job for very long. My lack of confidence and self-esteem kept me from being successful. What you believe about yourself is so important. You can overcome anything if you change your beliefs… especially your beliefs about yourself.

Pete, Margie, Patsy & Linda Bratcher

I am the youngest of my family and, yes, the most spoiled. I have two older sisters: Linda, who is two years older than me, and Patsy, who is four years older than me. I'm told that my parents brought me home from the hospital, laid me in a bassinet, then introduced me to my two sisters. They were not too happy about the arrival of the to-be-spoiled little boy. One of my sister's first reactions was to walk to my bassinet and throw metal Tonka trucks over the side…with me in it. Of course, I don't remember that, but I think psychologically I still have a scar. Just kidding.

My parents, Pete and Margie, were wonderful. I never heard an argument between them, although I'm sure there were some. Because of that, our home was a place where there was no visible conflict. If they had a problem with each other, they took it to their bedroom and worked it out there. Consequently there was a lot of compromise. I grew up in such a manner that I received little or no discipline whatsoever. When I said earlier I was spoiled, I meant it. No, or very little correction, meant that I ruled the home. Let me just say it: I was horrible.

I can remember as early as five years old that we would go to church as a family and I actually loved it. I loved the singing; I liked the preacher; I liked the way the church smelled. It was always something I looked forward to doing.

One Sunday after church, I was left to attend an event with all the other kids. I didn't want to go, so I simply took off walking. I was alone on the street by myself at five years old. When I got home I told my mother, "We won't be going back to that place." And guess what? I can't remember that we ever went back to church as a family again.

You see, my mom had this idea, that was driven by the pop psychology of the day, that taught you should always let a child do anything he or she wanted. I was without any discipline. So I spent my entire childhood screaming out for someone to tell me what was right and wrong, to teach me good values, to teach me how to act…and nobody did. So as I grew up I became a very selfish individual; the only thing that mattered to me was me. Did I like it? No, not at all.

Every child needs discipline; it's called love. My dad was a great dad. I never remember a moment in my life where I was afraid of my dad or where I doubted that he loved me. But what I needed most from my dad was for him to grab me by the nape of the neck and to tell me, "No."

As I grew into adolescence I kept getting

worse. At 13 years old I got caught stealing some wheels off a car and was put on probation. I had three things to do to fulfill my probation. One, I had to go to school. Two, I couldn't hang around with the guys I did the crime with; and three, I had to go to church. The state of Missouri mandated that I go to church. It was a different time for sure. I remember going to a little Baptist church in our neighborhood. I would sit as close to the door and as far away from the preacher as I could. Still today, I remember his sermons. They were simple, full of love and full of Jesus. I remember how badly I wanted to respond. I wanted to receive what he was talking about, but I was afraid of what my friends would think. So every week I rejected the message.

Finally off of probation, just a few months later I discovered LSD. It became my drug of choice and it was only a matter of time before I was using it on a regular basis. I was looking for an escape; I was looking for a way out. Anything to keep me from facing myself and the reality of who I was becoming. Of course, I didn't know that was what I was doing. And at that time in our culture, it seemed like it was the thing to do.

As one thing always leads to another, I went blindly down the path from one drug to another. At that time in my life I only had respect for two things: JB Rare scotch and heroin. I had enough respect for those two things that I would not use them regularly because I liked them so much, and I knew it would only be a matter of time before they would kill me.

I assumed that I would never make it past 25 years of age. I had this gnawing in my heart that said somehow, someway, I would die. You know, I had some crazy thought like, "Only the good die young." And somehow in my warped mind I thought that would bring the relief that I was looking for. I'm so glad that it didn't happen. I'm so glad that there was something in my path to stop me from taking that road. And that's what this story is all about.

One of the things I loved doing at this time in my life was watching TV preachers. I know that sounds crazy, but that's what I would do. I loved to take LSD and watch TV preachers. Catherine Kuhlman was my favorite, she was wild to watch. She was an old-school healing evangelist and she wore these flowing robes and would come out waving her arms in the air and saying, "I believe in miracles." I would just stare at the TV set and say, "WOW, man!" But even in all of my dysfunction I knew Jesus was real and somehow, someplace I would meet him.

So I say to you: Never give up hope; always look to Him. He's not waiting to approve you. He has *already* approved you. He is only waiting for you to open up your heart and say, "Help me."

It would take me many years to come to that place and to ask Jesus for His help. And I'm so glad that I did. If you haven't asked Him for His help, now is a really good time to ask.

CHAPTER TWO

Am I Hallucinating?

It was March 16, 1971, and I made my way to Memorial Hall in Kansas City, Kansas. I had just scored a couple of hits of LSD and was starting to come on (feel the effect). I made my way into the hall like all the other hippies. We were there to see the band Black Sabbath with their crazy lead singer Ozzy Osbourne. As I was finding my seat, in the crowd I spotted a friend, and as I got closer, behind him just out of my sight… there she was. She took my breath away. Now I joke that I didn't know if she was really that beautiful or if I was hallucinating! And yes, she is that beautiful. She didn't speak; we didn't talk. I went to my seat and that was it. But in the back of my mind, or the front of my heart, I knew there was something about this girl that I had to know.

Months passed and one summer day while parked in front of a local liquor store waiting for a friend, there she was. She walked right in front of my car. Again, we didn't speak. She didn't even know I was there, but something deep down in my heart was on fire. My friend came out of the liquor store and she walked off.

A few months later some of my band mates rented a house in Excelsior Springs, Missouri. We moved in and starting rehearsing and partying. When one day, in front of the house "*there she was just walking down the street.*" Then it happened! Late one evening as I was driving through downtown, there she was with one of my friends. So I asked, "You guys want a ride?" As we cruised around town, I invited Sherri to stop by our rehearsal house some time. After all, she just lived around the corner a few houses away.

Now, I'm the kind of guy that's completely oblivious to the whole flirting game. I mean, I was never any good at it…ever. Sherri would stop by the rehearsal house and one-by-one my band mates would hit on her (ask her out) and one-by-one she would shut them down. I will never forget one afternoon she stopped by, and again one the boys had hit on her; and like always, she'd shut him down. I was outside sitting on the front porch when he walked out and sat down beside me and said, "Can't you see what's going on here?"

"No."

"She is here for you!"

"Really?"

"Yes, she is!"

So finally her message made its way through

my thick head.

Let me tell you, it was a mess right from the beginning. From the start, the fighting began and didn't ever let up. I had grown up in a house where I had never heard my parents fight, but for Sherri it was just the opposite. Her parents fought pretty much all the time. So that was the only way she knew to express herself and deal with conflict. Couple that with my extreme selfishness and all that is left is for the announcer to say, "Let's get ready to rumble!"

I don't remember what we fought about, we just were really good at it and did it all the time. But now I know why we fought: I didn't know how to be a man and she didn't know how to be a woman. What I mean is, we didn't know how to treat ourselves or how to treat each other. We'd say anything and do almost anything to each other just as long as we got "our way." Confusion, and chaos was the atmosphere of our lives.

My response was to do what I knew how to

do best, hide. So I would simply leave the house "to go to the store," and disappear for days or weeks. But for some reason I would always come back. I felt so connected down deep in my heart to this girl that even though there was great pain, we just couldn't keep our hands off of each other. So you know how that works... it was just a few months and the announcement came, "I'm pregnant." Those were two words I wasn't ready to hear. But somehow, six months in, we managed to get a license and make an appointment with the judge.

The judge was late for court that morning, so he was put out that we wanted to get married; reluctantly he fulfilled his duties. It wasn't romantic—as a matter of fact, it was terrible. Afterwards we went to my aunt Evelyn's where she and my family had a reception for us. My family was very kind and was always trying to help us. But the help I needed most was to have someone to teach me how to be a man, someone to teach me how to be disciplined, someone to teach me how to care about someone other than myself.

So I started my life as a husband with a pregnant wife, no job, no money, no place to live—just the two of us and all of the chaos and conflict that we could produce. We ended up living at my parents' house in the basement, fighting constantly. It was like there was never an end to the conflict.

As Jimmie said, we first met at a Black Sabbath concert and he was such a sharp hippie dresser. He had on tan dingo boots, a wine-colored velour shirt with striped bell bottom pants…and man, oh man, I knew I wanted to know him! I heard someone say one time that when you fall in love, your brains fall out on the floor. And yes, for me, that's just what happened. It was probably lust rather than love, because we hadn't even spoken before.

I had seen him several times when he wasn't aware and never had the guts to pursue him. But when he moved around the corner from my folks' house, I decided I was gonna go for it… and boy what a mess! Before we met he was crazy, and I was just crazy somewhere else, and then we brought our crazies together. I wish I could tell you that this time in our lives wasn't bad, but it was. I truly believe that I was on a bend towards destruction. I, like Jimmie, didn't even think I would live to the age of 25 and truly didn't care if I did or not.

So as he said, when I was six months pregnant we got married by a justice of the peace, and it was awful! And now, here I was married to a man who didn't want me, and I'm pregnant! I didn't know anything about kids—nothing. I never was around any, and I sure felt like I wasn't allowed to be one. I was forced to grow up way too fast.

I know it was a gift that we were staying in Jimmie's parents' basement. But we sure brought a lot of crazy into their house. Fighting constantly! We were so young, wild, selfish, stupid and lost.

CHAPTER THREE

Round One

So here we are: the happy (NOT), nineteen year olds living in the basement of my folks' house. You know, those folks that never fought in front of their kids? Oh, yeah,...*those* folks. You can't imagine the chaos and confusion that Sherri and I brought into that environment.

It was crazy. We screamed, we yelled, and we fought about everything. Why? Well, looking back I would say it was all about our own personal selfishness. We each wanted things our way and if we didn't get our way, we fought. We had no boundaries and no one standing up to us and saying, "Knock it off!" and we didn't really even know what we wanted from life. So it continued. I hated it, Sherri hated it, our parents hated it, even our friends hated it. It was horrible.

As always, I responded the only way I knew how, I would hide. But at Pete and Margie's 900 square foot split-level, there was no place to hide. So my brilliant solution was to simply announce, "I'm going to the store to get some cigarettes." Days, sometimes weeks would pass before I would be seen again.

Where would I go? I would hide. Crashing on friends' couches; staying out partying as long as I could; scrounging the money to keep me in beer and cigarettes. What about clean clothes, what about food? Nothing mattered to me but finding a place where I got my way and didn't have to face my responsibilities. Finally, I would start feeling bad enough that I would come dragging my sorry butt back to Pete and Marge's to face my abandoned, pregnant wife, Sherri.

It would take some time for me to convince Sherri, and my mom and dad, that I could be trusted again. Before long they would give in and it was business as usual. We were fighting again. Sometimes it would be bad enough that Sherri would need to go to her parents' house so everyone could have some peace and quiet.

There were times I wanted to break away from Jimmie and just break away from life itself. So, sometimes I would leave with friends or go to my folks' house for a little while, but then I would be drawn right back into it all.

One time when I was pregnant, Jimmie and I were invited to a party on a farm outside of Liberty. There were lots of drugs and drinking available and Jimmie was taking advantage of that as I laid out by the pond and fell asleep. One by one everyone left, and I was still asleep for about five hours in the summer sun. When I woke up I was severely sunburned and in much pain. I got a ride home to Jimmie's folks' house and his mom realized how hurt and sick I was. I couldn't walk, my legs were throbbing, and anything touching my skin was way too painful to explain.

Jimmie was gone for days. I would lie in our bedroom and cry night after night, and to a degree during that time, I gave up believing that I was worth anything.

Our desire in writing about our painful past is that we hope it will bring you hope. That no matter how dark things are, it is never too dark that Jesus can't help! Thank God he came to seek and save us all!

I didn't know at the time that you should never expect anyone to fulfill you. I know now only God can bring that type of fulfillment and completion in your life. Colossians 2:10 says, *"you are complete in Him"*. Meaning that once we accept God's love in Christ Jesus, He then defines and completes us and we discover our true identity. People can bring added benefits to your life, but they can never be the totality of your life.

We had both done so many hurtful and harmful things to our bodies it was crazy. Just before we met, Sherri had been in the hospital because her body was damaged by all the abuse. Now she was pregnant. With all of the past abuse and now the strain on her body from carrying the baby, one day it hit me like a truck: What if the baby isn't healthy? What if the baby was deformed, not only from Sherri's abuse of her body, but mine, too?

Even though I didn't go to church, even though I didn't know Jesus, I would still ask God to make our baby healthy: "Lord, would you protect and heal our baby?" All the way up to birth, I prayed asking God to help and heal our baby. When our son, Jason, was born and I saw him for the first time, I checked his hands and feet to see if he was all there. He was a perfect little baby boy. As I held him in my arms I was so overwhelmed with thanks, I had to leave the room. I went and found a place where I could thank God that Jason was alright. I was so grateful that he had all his fingers and toes!

So you might say, "God doesn't hear those kind of prayers." To you I would say, "Well, I'm not God and neither are you, so shut up." Honestly I don't know if God heard my prayers, but I held in my arms a healthy baby boy and I simply wanted to give thanks to God for His wonderful gift to such an undeserving father.

A few weeks later at one of Jason's first visits to the doctor we heard the news that shook us. "Your son has Down Syndrome." The doctor pointed to his nose and said, "Look at his nose, there's no bridge. He is a Down Syndrome baby." The doctor told us he would know for sure by his next checkup. If you know anything about the Bratcher family, we are famous for our noses: well defined and big. But Jason didn't have any of those features.

You would have thought the doctor's words would have crushed us, but they didn't. We didn't know anything about faith. We didn't know Jesus as healer, but looking back at that time both Sherri and I had this determination in our hearts that said *he is not what the doctors say he is.* We had this confidence in our hearts that said our boy is fine. And that was that.

We went to Jason's next checkup and as the doctor was about to exit the room, Sherri asked, "Does he have Down Syndrome like the other doctor said?" He looked at us with a puzzling look and said, "No, he does not!"

I remember leaving the doctor's office and knowing in my heart that God did something for Jason and for a brief moment we were content and very, very thankful.

First Family Picture

Tulsa Time

One weekend I borrowed my dad's 1965 Chevy van and Sherri, Jason and I headed to Tulsa to party with some friends. We set up a playpen in the back of the van and Jason was crawling around in it and sitting on our lap at times, too. No car seat, no safety restraint, just a kid bouncing down the road in a hippy van with his crazy hippy parents. It was a different time for sure.

We got to Tulsa and liked it so much we decided to stay. No job, no money. We just crashed at some friends' apartment till they finally got sick of us and they moved out and left the apartment to us. They must have really been tired of us.

It was the first time Sherri and I had been on our own. It was the first time we were faced with each other. It was the first time I had no place to hide…no friends to run to. And for the first time things actually started to click. I found some work and somehow we managed to make it happen. We loved Tulsa but Tulsa didn't love us, or at least that's how it seemed. We arrived at the height of the oil crisis in the early '70s and jobs were very hard to find, so we struggled. But we had some wonderful times in Tulsa. Jason's first birthday, our first dog Waldo, and—most of all—Sherri and I were becoming husband and wife and we weren't fighting.

We had very little furniture and the rooms in our apartment were huge. Jason never really learned how to crawl. We would just throw one of his kids books on the floor and he would put his hands on it, start moving his legs and scoot around. And it was so funny because he never really learned how to walk either. Because the distance was so great between our few pieces of furniture, one day he just took off running. From then on that's what he did. He learned how to run before he could walk.

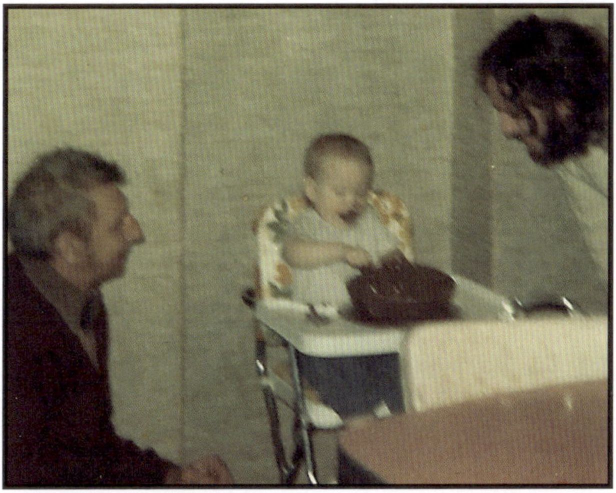

Jason's first birthday
Jimmie, Pete and Jason.

Times were hard and we just couldn't make ends meet. My sister Patsy flew down to visit one weekend, and before the weekend was over, we had decided to move back to Pete and Margie's. So on a very cold winter night, we loaded up our 1964 Ford station wagon and headed north.

I remember in a passing moment on the front lawn while loading the car, I said to Sherri, "If we move back to Kansas City we will get a divorce." At that moment it struck me so hard that I knew that it wouldn't be long and we would be divorced.

Today, I realize the power that words like that can have in our lives. And that is exactly what happened. Why? Well, there were a lot of reasons why we needed to be divorced. But today I know that our world is created by our words. We live where we live, drive the car we drive and are married to the person we are married to because we said something. Our words are so powerful.

I didn't understand how powerful the words I had spoken were. They were so powerful that they would soon be creating and shaping my world.

The drive back to Kansas from Tulsa was long and very cold. I really didn't want to move back to Kansas City because I felt that even though Jimmie had been having a hard time finding work, we as a couple, along with our baby boy, were beginning to build trust and were growing to depend on each other. It was the first time we experienced anything like this, and both of us knew it was a good thing. I knew that moving back would throw all of that into chaos.

When we got back to town we stayed a short time with Jimmie's parents. Soon afterwards, Jimmie, Jason and I moved into a small apartment in Pleasant

Valley, Missouri. While living there, my parents started having trouble in their on-again-off-again relationship and separated. My dad Elmer came to live with us for a short time before they were able to patch things up, yet again, and he moved back home. Having my dad living with us meant that we didn't fight as much, simply because he was there. The hard thing for me was that Jimmie began to fall back into his old habits, and Jason and I found ourselves alone more and more.

I mentioned earlier that I had made some personal constitutions or promises to myself that I would never allow a broken home to happen to me. But I had to come to realize that in every situation, God gives us the gift of choice and that we control the choices we make. I guess He could have made us all like puppets so we would do whatever He wants; but He wants us to choose Him and His way of doing things out of a heart of love and trust for Him.

One night as Jason was sleeping in the apartment, I walked outside and cried. I was so brokenhearted; I felt like I had lived such a worthless life. I felt I had no value and my self-worth was gone—if I ever even had any.

Across from where we lived there was a gully, and several yards past that was a big house. That night they were having a big party and I thought to myself, *I just don't want that life anymore.* I felt a peace come over me and I cried out to the Lord and all I could say was "Help me." I'm so thankful He heard me and He began to work. Even though it wasn't that apparent at first, He began putting roadblocks in my life—people who knew Jesus in a real way and had faith for our lives and our path to change. God is such a good, good Father!

Well, it soon became apparent that Jimmie didn't want to be with me, so we separated and moved out of the apartment in Pleasant Valley. The sad thing was I truly began to think that Jason would be better off without me and that I should leave him with Jimmie's mom and dad—at least there he would have a stable place. They loved him so much, and he brought them so much joy! I went to Pete and Margie's house once more just to try to convince Jimmie that we could make it, but it was over. I was so devastated by it all and that night I tried to take my own life by slitting my wrist. I could see no future or hope for me.

Jimmie's folks called my parents to come get me. I couldn't bear to move back with my folks so I ended up moving in with a single mom and her son. It was way out in the country and I had no car, no job, no running water; it wasn't a very fun place at all and I found myself alone again.

CHAPTER FOUR

Granny Pays for the Divorce

One night I heard Jimmie was playing in a band at a local bar and Jason was staying with Jimmie's parents. My friend and I went to hear them and I ended up leaving with Jimmie. We had both been drinking, and on the way he informed me that he was not going to take me back to his parents' house to get Jason. We began to argue intensely and he took me back to my place to drop me off. I was desperate so I told him, "You will take me to get Jason or else I will get in the back of this truck and stomp all of your guitars to bits!" I jumped out of the truck, ran around the back, got up in the bed and started to kick things. Now, you must understand that we used to fight so much and so hard, we never knew how far it would escalate.

By now Jimmie was standing at the back of the truck, he reached out and grabbed one of my legs, sat me down and started to pull me out of the bed of the truck. We were both so mad! I was just trying to get him away from me, so I cocked back my other leg and kicked him—my foot hit right on his nose.

I wasn't aiming for it but that's where it hit. I had hiking boots on that night; we used to call them "waffle stompers" because of the pattern they made in the snow when you walked in them. Needless to say, his nose did not take the hit very well, the fight stopped and he headed out in a hurry. So watch out for me if I'm wearing waffle stompers!

The next day at the ER the doctor said, "You need reconstructive surgery on your nose." I couldn't believe it. It was causing me much pain and I was not able to breathe properly through it. He said my nose was S shaped. Now, before I discovered drugs and alcohol I was a baseball player, big time, and I'd been hit in the nose with baseballs many, many times and for sure my nose looked like an S. So surgery was scheduled.

Upon being released from the hospital I went home to my parents' house to recover and at that time my grandmother—"Granny"—was staying there. Now, Granny was some kind of woman; I mean she was really tough. She grew up in a less-than-ideal setting—in fact it was very abusive—but if you talked to her you would never hear anything about it. She was always kind to me, but I knew you didn't want to mess with Granny. She just had this look like it was tattooed on her forehead: "Mess with me and I will hurt you." But I knew Granny was a sweetheart. Or maybe I just knew that Granny would do pretty much anything for me because she loved me.

She came in as I was lying on the couch and saw me. My eyes were black way down to my cheeks and I still had packs in my nose from the surgery. Needless to say, I was a mess. She sat down on the couch next to me and said these words, "Baby, I will give you the money if you will just get a divorce." Now you know that your marriage is jacked up when Granny is willing to pay for your divorce.

In a few days, after I recovered, I was off to the attorney's office. Sherri and I split up our few belongings and agreed that we would share custody of Jason. Then we waited for our day in court.

Jimmie & Granny

CHAPTER FIVE

I'm Divorced, and I Don't Fit Anywhere

I remember it was a bright spring day as I walked into the courthouse, and there she was—my wife; alone, abused and brokenhearted. The pain was so great for each of us, but we had to take these steps. We knew—and I think everyone else knew—if we didn't divorce, one of us could end up dead, and no one wanted that. So the judge granted our divorce and we went our separate ways.

Before I start writing about our divorce let me say this: Sherri and I have the utmost respect for single parents. In fact, they are some of our biggest heroes! Before we discuss this part of our life, we always like to speak directly to single parents and those who find themselves divorced. This is what we tell them: *You are not insufficient.* Ask God for the wisdom it takes for you to be single; and if you have children, ask God for the wisdom it takes to raise them, and He will give it to you.

One sure promise from the Bible is that if you "*lack wisdom, He will give it and He will give it liberally.*" (James 1:5) I know many, many wonderful adults who were raised by single parents and they are absolutely outstanding individuals. So don't ever think of yourself as less than enough or, as I said earlier, "insufficient." You and Jesus are always enough and more than capable to do the job. Colossians 1:20 says, *"You are complete in Him."*

Being divorced is hard. It is one of the hardest, most violent things that I've ever done in my life. I saw the violent effect on my son and the rest of my family. It takes a strong—very strong—power to separate what God has joined together. It can be done, but it is very hard and it is very difficult for a reason.

Of course, I didn't know that God had joined anything together in my marriage, yet He had. All I knew was that the pain was so great and that we had to do something to keep from hurting each other and Jason. It seemed that divorce was the only way, and at the time, it *was* the only way.

Looking back on that moment of our day in court, my emotions were all over the road. I was relieved for the chaos to stop, but at the same time I *was* very sad. I remember when we said our last goodbye on the steps of the Liberty, Missouri, courthouse and walked away. I thought that was the end of that, and in a sense it *was* the end.

What I didn't know was that something

supernatural had taken place when Sherri and I said our vows to each other when we were first married. Since we didn't know the Lord, I had no idea that He was involved in our marriage. But I was in for a huge shock.

I began to run as fast and as hard as I could into a crazy party lifestyle. I was working a job as an electrician and I would party all night, every night. Then my boss would pick me up on the way to the job and my hungover self would go to work. I am sure it was awful for anyone to be around me at that time. I would drink like there was no tomorrow, stumble home about four o'clock in the morning, get up at seven and head to work.

All of that time was about one thing: numbing the pain and quieting the conflicting voices in my head. No, I didn't want to be married to Sherri, but at the same time, whenever I would pursue a relationship with someone else, it just didn't feel right. I would take a girl out and somehow in my heart I knew it was not right. It didn't have anything to do with that person, there was something inside of me that was crying out. Today I know what it was, so let me explain.

You see, marriage is God's idea. It is something that He created and that He loves. One of the first things the Bible tells us about marriage is found in Genesis 2:24 and it says, "*This explains why a man leaves his father and mother and is joined to his wife, and the two are united into one.*" (NLT) When you study the word 'joined' in this passage you find that it means "adhesive or glue." This is what happens when we are married. We are joined or glued together in such a way that the Bible says "*we are united into one.*" I relate to it like this:

Elmer's Glue is a fabulous adhesive, especially when working with wood. I have an old guitar that I dropped and broke into pieces, then my dad and I glued it back together back in 1967 using Elmer's Glue. To this day that glue is still holding! In woodworking when you glue two pieces of wood together and then separate them, (which isn't easy) they don't separate clean. Pieces from one will be on the other. So if you try to place either piece of wood with another piece of wood they just won't fit. That is exactly what I was experiencing emotionally. Everywhere I would try to fit, I knew in my heart that I just didn't fit there.

This is also why I believe you see couples separate then get back together, separate and get back together. It's a crazy cycle that seems to make no sense. There may even be abuse in the relationship. Everyone in their family is pleading with them to please stay apart. But as crazy as it is, they come back together.

While Sherri and I were divorced, there were a few times when we slept together. It was insane, even though both of us knew it was over. Every time it would happen in my heart I would know: *This is where I belong, she is the one I am supposed to be with.* I didn't want to face it at the time, but I knew it just felt right, and I couldn't escape the feeling I experienced being with her.

SHERRI

Jimmie and I want to make sure to clarify that if you have been divorced and you have remarried other people, God is not against you, He is for you. In any marriage relationship both parties must be dedicated to the success of the marriage. One person cannot hold the full responsibility for keeping it together if the other wants out of it. So please understand that if you are remarried, then your current marriage is the one the Lord wants to succeed!

> "You are not insufficient."

Also, we do want to clarify that if there is abuse in your relationship, get help and be wise. Please understand, if your life or your children's lives are in danger, get out and get help fast! DO NOT try to do it on your own. If you are in an abusive relationship, your judgements may not clear. You may need someone (a counselor or pastor) to help you see the actions that you need to take. There isn't any shame in having a problem, there is only shame if there is help available and you don't go get it.

Divorce is something that is talked about in the Bible. Malachi 2:16 says: *"The man who hates and divorces his wife," says the LORD, the God of Israel, "does violence to the one he should protect," says the LORD Almighty. So be on your guard, and do not be unfaithful."* (NIV) Divorce is a violent act and there is no way round it. The Bible explains why God hates divorce in Malachi 2:15: *"Has not the one God made you? You belong to him in body and spirit.*

> "God is not against you, He is for you."

And what does the one God seek? Godly offspring. So be on your guard, and do not be unfaithful to the wife of your youth." (NIV) God hates divorce because He seeks "godly offspring." He hates divorce because of the effects it has on everyone, especially the children. Whenever there is hate involved in divorce it is devastating on everyone, but mostly on the kids. We adults have had the time to learn how to protect ourselves from the effects of hate, but the children have not. One of my preacher friends describes it like this, "God hates the hateful divorce."

Divorce is however a law, that God allowed to be put in the Bible. He added it to the law, therefore it is a legitimate option that is there to protect us. There are times when divorce is the best option in a relationship and many times it is what saves the children from having lifelong emotional damage. I know it was the best option at the time for Sherri and me.

Jesus taught about divorce. When the leaders

of His day asked Him this question in Matthew 19:3: *Some Pharisees came to him to test him. They asked, "Is it lawful for a man to divorce his wife for any and every reason?"* (NIV) Jesus answered their question like this in verse 6: *"Therefore what God has joined together, let no one separate."* (NIV) They then responded in verse 7: *"Why then," they asked, "did Moses command that a man give his wife a certificate of divorce and send her away?"* In the next statement Jesus reveals what is the "root issue" in every relationship problem. In verse 8: Jesus replied, *"Moses permitted you to divorce your wives because your hearts were hard. But it was not this way from the beginning."*

A hard-hearted person has closed the door to love and is not capable of giving or receiving love. Love is the hallmark emotion of planet earth and it transcends throughout eternity. A person with a hard heart has closed the door on fully experiencing love. Many times it is from a hateful relationship from the past or childhood. Many times we have simply never really experienced or felt the love that God has for us, and therefore we cannot really trust anyone with our hearts. Trust is the root of all things Godly. Trust opens our hearts to experience love. God loves us first and because of His love, we in turn, can trust Him and love Him.

So what can you do with a hard and broken heart? Give it to the One who can heal it and watch what happens.

> "Trust is the root of all things Godly.
> Trust opens our hearts
> to experience love."

CHAPTER SIX

My First Invitation... Small Breakthroughs

One day, Jason and I were in a store in Excelsior Springs, and I saw a lady whom I'd met at a church service where Jimmie's sister, Patsy, had taken me. Her name was Jeannie and she was a very normal, loving wife and mom. She had four kids and her face lit up when she saw me! Our worlds were so far apart, but she was very kind. My head went down when I saw her, but she just kept coming, and she said to me, "Sherri, I have been thinking about you!" I was shocked! I thought to myself, *Really? You've been thinking about me?* It was so great because if she had judged me by my outward appearance, she might have just passed me by. The cool thing is I had prayed the night before—just a simple prayer: "God if you are out there, I want to know you!" I believe that God hears prayers like that one.

> "If she had judged me by my outward appearance, she might have just passed me by."

She began to tell me about where they were going to church and how much they loved it. She asked if they could come and pick me up the next morning and wanted to know if I would spend the day with them at this church. I was so reluctant at first, but then I said yes. So the next morning, bright and early, they came to get us for church in their old station wagon. The funny thing was that Jimmie had been coming back around again, but we couldn't tell anybody. Our parents would have had us locked up, and Granny would have wanted her money back.

The previous evening Jimmie was supposed to come and pick Jason and me up for a date, but he didn't show up. Jason cried himself to sleep and I was so furious. My heart wasn't willing to take any more pain. It had rained hard that night and Jimmie had gone out partying instead. He was drinking scotch and doing amphetamines when his car broke down in a torrential downpour outside of town and he ended up walking to my house. When he got there around 4 a.m., I was not glad to see him. So morning came and Jeannie and her family were supposed to arrive at 7 a.m. to get Jason and me. When they got there (and to my surprise) Jimmie, Jason and I went with them. Jimmie had to sit in the back facing out of their station wagon…you know the seat facing out the back window? It was so funny, and he was all hungover and miserable.

When we arrived at the church, the very first person I saw, was one of my old drug dealers and I thought to myself, *What kind of church is this?* We ended up being there all day long. The great thing about it was these people had no motive but to love us, and kept telling us of the love God had for us. It was a truly moving experience and we both felt something! At the end of the day the preacher asked, "If you would like to know more about Jesus, raise your hand." The only hand raised was Jimmie's.

Yes, he received prayer, but when we got back to my house things went downhill. The fighting, the drugs, and the hiding. It was business as usual for Jimmie.

Jason and I continued to go to church and heard how God had a fresh start for us. We began to feel God was pursuing us. Jason had that innocent faith. He was all in, but I would go week after week and hear the message and think, *oh, I wish that could be for me.* I was so full of shame that it took a while before I could actually believe. My breakthroughs were small, but with every beam of light that found a crack in my hardened heart, the light would explode. I am so thankful He didn't give up on me. He just kept drawing me.

Jeanie consistently came to get Jason and me for church until I got a car. It was a navy blue Chevy Corvair. (I wish I still had it!) This is the type of car Jimmie taught me how to drive a stick shift in. He had taken me to the highest hill in Clay County, Missouri, parked it going uphill, got out and said, "If you can take it from here, you can drive anywhere." I loved that car and loved driving it!

Okay, back to going to church. I can't begin to put into words the love I was experiencing. I was hearing over and over again how Jesus loved me and wanted to give me a new start. I was so brokenhearted and full of shame when I first came to church. It took quite a while for my faith to come alive, but I loved what I was hearing. It was creating hope in me for the first time. The people there knew I was jacked up, but still gave me the same privilege they had of sitting and hearing the word of God so that faith could come. They were not judgmental, but loved Jason and me and modeled for us what our life and our future could be like. It was remarkable. My eyes were seeing clearer and clearer every time I heard the Good News.

I had several wonderful ladies helping me, praying for me, teaching me and loving me. I was going to a Bible study, but this kind of thing was all new to me. One night while taking on the phone to one of the ladies whom I respected greatly, she asked me, "Sherri what are your plans now that you have met the Lord?" I answered her like this: "Well, my life is all messed up and Jesus loves me, so I'm gonna believe He will save Jimmie and put our marriage back together." Her response shocked me and made me angry! She said, "Well, you just better get another plan. Jimmie is not the type to be saved!" What?! I got off the phone and I said to the Lord, "Really, he's not the type to be saved? My life is all jacked up and his is too, but you will save me but not him? What do you say about that Lord?"

So in innocent faith, I flipped open my Bible and slammed my finger down on the page and this is the verse I read: *"They replied, "Believe in the Lord Jesus and you will be saved, along with everyone in your household."* Acts 16:31 (NLT). Then I said out loud, "Well then, that's what I'm gonna believe!" There were lots of occasions after this that created doubt in my life, but Jason and I just kept going to church. We just kept hoping and believing. I didn't really know if I was saved or not, but I knew the Lord was after me, pursuing me, bringing good things into my broken life.

Jason & Sherri

CHAPTER SEVEN

The Power of a Little Boy

Jason was the only bright spot in my life. After the divorce I moved in with my best friend and my substance abuse just got worse. But I had joint custody of Jason so whenever he was with me I would keep things down to a mild roar. By now Sherri had started taking Jason to church and Sunday School. One night Jason was at my house and some friends were there partying, too. My friends were drinking and smoking dope in the other room while Jason and I sat on the couch. As the party continued, out of the blue, Jason just started singing some of the songs he'd learned in Sunday School. It only took a few minutes before the house was totally empty. Jason and his Sunday School songs cleaned the place out. It was some kind of moment. I remember thinking, *I should tell him to stop singing those songs.* But what was that going to teach him? I just couldn't bring myself to say anything. So we spent the evening alone. Me being so convicted and miserable, and Jason happily singing Sunday School songs.

I didn't know the power that a little boy's songs could have. Today, I know that it was Jesus trying to reach me and my friends and He was using Jason to do it.

A few weeks later I'd made a date with Sherri and Jason, and as the time came to pick them up, I didn't call. I just didn't show up. Hiding is what I did best back then. After a night of drinking and taking

Jason

amphetamines (speed), my guilt over what I had done got the best of me. So about 2 a.m. I made the drunken, drugged drive from Kansas City to Excelsior Springs, which is about 30 miles. Just as I was pulling into town, my car quit…oh, and it was raining. Like thunderstorm-type raining. Sounds like a blues song doesn't it?

You have to remember this was way before mobile phones and it wouldn't have even mattered because Sherri didn't have a phone at all. So I took off walking. I don't remember if I walked all the way or not. Let's just say that when I arrived at Sherri's about 4:00 a.m., I was drenched and she was not at all happy to see me. So I did what I always did, I started trying to weasel my way out of the mess I'd made. "What are you and Jason doing tomorrow?"

"We are going to church," she said.

"Well, I'll go with you!"

Seven o'clock the next morning came and needless to say, I was in no shape to go anywhere. So I flooded Sherri with excuses and none of them seemed to work. So she gathered up Jason's things and headed out the door. I still remember the sound of that door slamming as they left. So I grabbed my wet jacket and out the door I went after them.

There it was, a dirty Ford station wagon full of kids and only one seat left for me: the one in the very back that faced out the back of the car. Hungover and not really wanting to go, this was just wonderful. So I crawled in, and off to God's Sheep Shed we went. I thought, *Hey! this will just take a couple of hours right?* No, it was an all day, all evening deal. Fabulous! And it rained all day.

God's Sheep Shed was really nothing more than a shelter house in the middle of an 80-acre farm. You know, a shelter house like you would see in a city park—just a roof with some poles holding it up. But as winter approached walls were built to block the wind, the floor was dirt and for heat there was a wood stove in the middle of the room. I loved it. It was crude, raw, unfinished and just perfect for me.

We arrived and this tall, overwhelming, smiling man came up to me. His hands were rough and huge, his smile infectious and he had a very charismatic personality. "I'm Ray," he said, wrapping me up in a huge bear hug. He was the pastor. Needless to say I was more than intimidated, but at the same time felt something. There was something in the air…it was magnetic, and I liked it. If I could only overcome the fear I felt. It was the same fear that I felt when I was 13 and on probation and forced to go to church. It was the fear of losing my friends—most of which had never really done anything to help me. It was the fear of losing my own self-image. Even as jacked up as my life was, I thought I still had something worth protecting. How messed up is that?

As the day went on and on, one by one the people there treated Sherri and me like they were happy we were there. They fed us, they talked to us, they treated us like we belonged, like we were part of the family. Now, being from a big family and always loving our massive family reunions, I knew what that feeling was like. As a kid, our family reunions were huge. My dad had eleven brothers and sisters, and when all of them would get together once every summer, it was something special. It was one of my most favorite times of the year. This day felt just like that. Like a family getting together and just being family. Nothing to prove, no agenda, just family enjoying each other. Everyone there made us feel like we were important. Which is something that we rarely ever felt.

During the evening meeting the man preaching asked, "Is there anyone here who would like to know more about Jesus? Raise your hand." It took a while but eventually my hand was in the air. He prayed and the meeting was over. Before we headed back to Sherri's, Ray told Sherri, "Jimmie's hand was the only hand raised." He told her to hang on to her hope and encouraged her to not kick me to the curb and just go on with her life.

One evening Jason and I were at church, and the pastor closed the evening service by saying, "Maybe you are here tonight and you are going through a rough time, and you want us to join our faith with yours. Come forward and let's pray together." Well, everything in me wanted to go forward for prayer, but I was still so full of shame and fear I couldn't move. Then I felt a tug on my shirt. It was Jason, he said, "Momma, we need prayer!" I replied, "I know we do Baby, but Jesus is gonna take care of us."

The pastor made the plea again, "Maybe you are here tonight and you are going through a rough time, and you want us to join our faith with yours. Come forward and let's pray together." Everything in me wanted to go but I was frozen by the shame, when again Jason said, "Momma, Momma, we need prayer." I replied, "I know Baby, so let's pray right here." As I reached down to pray with him, he said, "No, Mom. I want to go up there and pray." He meant up there at the altar, in public. So, reluctantly for just a moment, I left my shame and fear in my seat, took his hand, and we went forward to have prayer.

"Jason, what do you want Jesus to do for you?" Jason replied, "I want Jesus to bring my daddy home."

I told Pastor Ray that it was Jason who wanted prayer. So he got down on one knee, bent over and asked, "Jason, what do you want Jesus to do for you?" Jason replied, "I want Jesus to bring my daddy home." So we all prayed. I'm not sure if anyone had as much faith in that prayer as Jason did that night, but because he was so young, it was easy to know his faith was a simple, childlike faith. He was simply putting his trust in Jesus.

I had raised my hand and prayed in church, and then with Jason praying for me, somehow the seed was planted in my heart. Never think that a seed isn't powerful, because it has incredible power. Ever see a plant growing up through a crack in a sidewalk? How does that happen? It's just that powerful. Little did I know that seed would begin to work in my heart. It was so subtle, but oh, so powerful. I began to see things differently; I began to feel things differently. The appeal of, or the appetite I had for, destruction didn't have the same power that it had before. Most of all, in my heart I knew this whole Jesus deal was right.

Or maybe it was just my conscience? But now I know it was the voice of the Holy Spirit showing Jesus to me. The voice was never condemning; it was a kind voice, and I knew I should follow it—no questions about that. The problem was I had never followed through on anything…ever. There was not one part of my life that I ever completed or finished. Let's just say I was a quitter, and I knew I didn't have what it would take to pull this off. And I was right…I didn't.

Yet, inside of my heart there was this knowing, and I couldn't doubt it. I knew somehow some way, at some time in my life, I was going to know Jesus. I was going to experience what it was like to be forgiven. I was going to be a man; I was going to be a husband to Sherri and a father to my son. I just knew it *would happen.* How? It was beyond me, but I just knew it. I guess it was faith when I raised my hand that night at God's Sheep Shed. I guess when God saw my hand in the air, He knew what my heart was crying out for. With all the things *I didn't know,* I *did* know that something was happening inside of me. Even though I would fight it. Even though I would still hide and drink to calm the internal conflict. Even though I didn't have all the answers, I still knew.

CHAPTER EIGHT

Don't Tell Granny

I'd sold my favorite Gibson Les Paul guitar and used the money to buy some new instruments, a Fender Telecaster (which I still own) and a Sho Bud Pedal Steel Guitar. They were the tools needed to play country music, which at the time was really deeply speaking to me. George Jones, Buck Owens, Ronnie Milsap, Connie Smith and Mel Tillis all spoke to right where I was living. I got the wardrobe, the boots, the western shirt, western cut leather jacket. I had everything but the hat! It would have messed up my signature curly hair, and you know we couldn't have that.

The music spoke to me because it so strongly related to my life, and even more to my pain. It encouraged my drinking and everything else that was wrong. Sherri and I continued to see each other off and on. Most of the time when we were together we still fought. But still we had this thing inside of us that kept drawing us back to each other.

One night I had this crazy idea: "Let's get married again." When the words came out of my mouth I thought, *Have you lost your mind?* Nothing had changed, nothing was different in any way. Why would I think that getting married again would do anything? I thought it was a mistake, but it was too late now. I'd already said the words and I think that both of us knew it would be best for Jason if we stayed together. But not if we continued fighting and living the way we were.

We talked about it and I did what I'd always done…nothing. I put it off as long as possible and of course, we couldn't tell anyone—especially Granny. But finally we made it to the North Kansas City Hospital, got our blood test, and headed to the Liberty Missouri Courthouse to get the license. As we walked into the courthouse it felt like everyone in the place was watching us. I walked up to the counter, put down the cash and there it was, a marriage license.

So now what? I knew I wouldn't be going back to the judge that married us before. I told Sherri, "I want 'that preacher' to marry us this time," speaking about Pastor Ray. So we made a plan to head to God's Sheep Shed the next Sunday evening.

December 15, 1976, the day before it all changed.

Man! It was it cold. Like subzero nonsense. So whiskey was the drink of choice for a cold day. I started drinking about 11 a.m. and went hard after it till the evening. My roommate Randy's girlfriend was having a party and somehow I drove my drunken self there. I remember parking my car and making the walk into the apartment. The place was packed with friends and they were doing what my friends did, partying.

I made it once around the room found the whisky and a huge glass, mixed a drink and found a seat. I emptied that glass, then mixed another one. From then on I only remember a few things. I remember stumbling back to my car in the freezing cold. I remember knowing that I was too drunk to drive, but I couldn't just pass out in the car or I would freeze to death. So I started the car and drove away.

I remember turning onto I-35 north and that is all I remember from the drive home. I woke up December 19th and I was home, in my bed, and hurting.

The Day It Happened

Every day always looks the same. You can't ever tell which day is going to be significant because they all make their appearance the same way, and this day was no different. I had no idea what December 19th would be in my life. I had no idea that today would be the day that my *change* would happen.

So many people had written me off as being beyond help—including myself. I wanted to be a man. I wanted to be a good husband and a good father. I wanted to change. I simply didn't have the power to do any of it, and the most shocking part was that *I knew it.*

I was very much aware of my weaknesses, but I didn't know what to do. Maybe someone somewhere could help me. Maybe someone would look into my life and find someone good. Maybe they could see hope for a future for me. Maybe they someone could see *a man.* I needed power and I needed it bad.

I Won't Join That Mess Together

I went and picked up Sherri and Jason, loaded up the car I had borrowed from my dad, and made the 40 mile drive to God's Sheep Shed. Since winter had set in, The Sheep Shed had some new improvements like a concrete floor, indoor plumbing and central heat. It was still primitive and I still loved it.

The first person I saw as we walked in the door was Pastor Ray. I reached into my pocket, pulled out the marriage license, and said, "We've got a marriage license and we want you to marry us tonight." I could tell by the look on his face that I wasn't going to like his answer, as he said, "Look, you're an alcoholic, drug addict and this young lady is trying to serve the Lord. I won't join that mess together." I'm sure I looked stunned, but I knew he was right. So we just found a seat and waited for the service to start.

A few minutes passed and Pastor Ray found me and said, "Alright I will marry you if you promise me that you will know Jesus." In my mind I thought, talk is cheap and I don't mind lying, so I agreed saying, "For sure, I will promise you that." He walked off saying, "Give me just a minute."

When he returned he said, "I will make an announcement during church that there will be a wedding after the service. We will give the folks a short break, then Brother Bob will sing a song. I will say a few things, we will do your vows, then I want to pray over you and I want you to kneel. Then you're going to believe on Jesus, is that okay?" My response was in typical hippie fashion, "Hey, man, I'm here." Which being interpreted meant "yes."

I remember sitting on the front row after church waiting for all this to take place and thinking, "Nothing changes. Tomorrow will be just like yesterday. I will do all the things I want to do and nothing will change." I really believed that is the way things would be. Then the time came.

Brother Bob sang his song. Then Pastor Ray said a few words, none of which I remember. He asked us to kneel, prayed over us and then said, "Jimmie, it's time for you to come to Jesus." Suddenly I was overtaken by emotion. Tears flooded my eyes and I heard myself talking to Jesus, asking Him to help me, asking Him to forgive me.

In that moment—which to this day is still as fresh in my heart as the day it happened—I knew I was different. I knew something had happened, something changed. I didn't know what. I didn't know how. I just knew. I had come face-to-face with real power. Not just any power, but the power of perfect love. I was stunned, shocked, amazed and I felt alive for the first time ever. I knew this is what I'd been looking for my whole life. I felt clean on the inside. I had never felt anything like it. I just knew I wanted it, I wanted to know Jesus and His wonderful Father who accepted me, "just as I am."

CHAPTER NINE

Transformation

When our wedding ceremony was over and we finally made it up off our knees, Pastor Ray asked us to face each other. He looked at me and said these words, "Jimmie, do you see Sherri? She doesn't have a past.

> "Jimmie, do you see Sherri?
> She doesn't have a past."

Because 2 Corinthians 5:17 says: *Therefore, if anyone is in Christ, he is a new creation; old things have passed away; behold, all things have become new."* Then he turned to Sherri and said the exact same words concerning me. It was life changing!

I have found nothing in my life as powerful as the power of forgiveness. In the Bible, to forgive means send away, to cut loose, to let go. One thing for sure, Sherri and I needed to send a boatload of stuff away. We could have filled a whole fleet of boats with all the things we needed to cut loose from our lives. Forgiveness was waiting for us to make the call and put it to work.

Although we were just married, we still had some unfinished business—like signing the marriage license. Pastor Ray invited us to his house which was only a few feet away from The Sheep Shed.

It was freezing outside and I remember stepping into Ray's house to find a huge fire in the fireplace. The house was warm and it was a beautiful earth contact home. Sherri and I sat down on the couch facing the fireplace; Ray and his wife Carla came in and we starting talking. I don't remember much about our conversation, but what I do remember is one thing that Carla said to me. When she said it, it was like I was hearing the words with my entire life, not just with my ears or even with my mind. It was like God was talking to me. I didn't know what that was like or how it should sound, but what she said hit me like a freight train. Carla was from middle Tennessee and she had a really thick southern drawl. We were just simply talking when she said these words: "Jimmie, now you're going to be in church all the time aren't you?" Bam, it hit me! "Well, yeah!" I said.

Even though I was still reeling from what had just happened (and actually still hungover from the night before), I knew that those words and my response would be pivotal to our future. After all, we were all jacked up and suddenly we found something that made sense, something that offered us help and a future. So, my answer was, "Yes. We will be in church all the time from now on." I made good on that and every time the doors were open, off to The Sheep Shed we would go. I can't tell you how deeply this affected our family.

Now, it wasn't like The Sheep Shed was just around the corner from our house—it was 40 miles away and we survived on a very limited budget. Shoot, we didn't even own a car at the time. At the time we were either driving one of my band member's extra cars or something I borrowed from my dad. And really, up to this point, I couldn't even keep a job. So the prospect of driving 80 miles roundtrip to church just was crazy.

But something wonderful had just happened and we knew that if we didn't learn more, we wouldn't make it. Our logic was that if we don't make the trip—if we don't make the commitment—in a few weeks or months we'll just be right back in the same place we were before. I needed someone to teach me how to be

a man, how to be a husband, and how to be a father.

Later that evening, as Sherri, Jason and I arrived back home at her grandmother's house where we were staying, we put Jason to bed. Sherri was tired so she went to bed and left me alone in the living room. The house was a very tiny four-room house with a free-standing gas heater in the middle of the living room. I remember lying on the floor still stunned from what had just happened. Then my eyes found a little picture of Jesus that her grandmother must have left hanging on the wall. It was one of those pictures of Jesus with a flaming heart. I remember pointing up to that picture and saying these words, "For the first time, I am at peace with You." I didn't know what to say or the right way to say it, but none of that mattered.

What did matter was that I knew in my heart that I had been accepted by God, loved by Jesus, and I was forgiven…and I just wanted to give thanks.

When I left The Sheep Shed that night, I was different. I couldn't explain it, I didn't understand it, but I knew in my heart something powerful had happened to me. And whatever it was, it was something I had longed to feel, longed to experience my entire life. To try to put it in words I would just say it like this:

I was at peace for the first time ever. Peace with myself, peace with Sherri, and most of all I knew I was at peace with God. Being a hippie I had always been in pursuit of peace, I will confess that I am a Peace Freak. And now, out of nowhere, I was blindsided by the most powerful peace I had ever felt. I experienced moments of peace at times while drinking and taking drugs, but never anything like this.

Telling Granny

Well, we were remarried and born again, but one big thing remained: telling our friends, family and oh, yeah…Telling Granny! Needless to say, we were stressing about that.

Our friends just thought we were crazy. They knew, all too well, how passionately we fought and how miserable we were. They just wrote us off as hopeless, then add in the Jesus factor and they figured we'd lose it for sure.

Our parents were reluctant, to say the least. Sherri's folks didn't really have much to say. My folks were happy, yet skeptical. All of them were hopeful… yet, without saying it, I could feel their doubt. None of them at that time were religious, (except for my sister Patsy) so no one really knew what to think about us becoming "Jesus Freaks."

Granny, on the other hand, was different. We

joke about not telling her because we were afraid that she'd want a refund, but I remember coming face-to-face with her in the living room at my folks' house. I shared the exciting news with her about us being remarried and that we had been saved. I watched the countenance of her face light up with a huge smile and she said, "Baby, that's what I've been praying for."

I started a new job washing cars at a Ford dealer in Kansas City, Kansas. When my first break came, the guy working next to me walked over and said, "I've got some drugs in the car if you want to get high!" Now normally I would have said, "Hell, yes!" but this time something was different. I stopped and considered his offer and said, "No, man. I've found something better than that." He looked puzzled and walked off to get high.

I went to band rehearsal that evening and there were drugs and drinks everywhere and for some reason I just didn't want it anymore. It just didn't appeal to me like it had only a few the hours before. Normally,

I would have been the one that would have been all over that stuff. I was always the one to start the party, to crack open a cold beer, or light up a joint…but not this time. It only took a few rehearsals like that and my band mates knew something was up with Jimmie.

I didn't know what to say about what had happened to me. I didn't know the right words to use, I only knew that my destructive desires had changed in a moment. The things I was searching for, the fulfillment I longed to know, was suddenly alive and real inside of me. It was just like the song "Amazing Grace." "I once was lost, but now I'm found, was blind but now I see." Everything was different. I didn't know how to say it, but I was born again.

Before December 19, 1976, I remember having angry conversations with Sherri about going to church or coming to Jesus. I would always say, "If I ever do something like that, I want to do it all the way. No holding back, no compromise. I will not be a hypocrite." Like I had some kind of power to actually make it happen. Every time I would say that, I could hear my conscience saying, "Yeah right, sure you will." I knew there was no way I could change anything in my life. I had tried; I had good intentions; I would use all my willpower. Yet, in just a few days or maybe weeks I would be right back doing the same thing over again. Maybe this time it would be different? And it was.

CHAPTER TEN

The DNA of a Quitter

Jimmie and I were both drastically changed on December 19,1976, and it was amazing. I felt the weight of guilt and shame fall off of me and knew I was free! When we walked away from that altar that night we were different! We went home that night knowing we were different, but also knew we had to walk it out. When Pastor Ray had us look at each other, and when he quoted 2 Corinthians 5:17, I realized we could start new. I realized that neither one of us had a past. That was such powerful stuff! Little did I know it would be tested and tried so quickly.

Jimmie was still playing in a band and one night shortly after Jesus transformed our world, Jimmie had a gig (band date) and thought he would be home by a certain time. But events changed that he had no control over and he was going to be much later getting home than he had originally thought.

At the time, we lived next door to my mom and dad in my grandmother's house and we didn't have a phone. So, doing the right thing and so I wouldn't worry, Jimmie called my mom and dad's house to ask them to go over and tell me what was going on. My folks didn't see a light on so they assumed I was asleep and they didn't come over to tell me he had called.

There I sat, awake in the living room, Jason was asleep and I began to cry as all those hurtful memories of Jimmie not coming back home for weeks flooded my heart and mind. I said to the Lord, "Jesus if this is how it's gonna be, then I am not willing to go through this anymore. My heart can't take it. How can I trust him again?" I heard a voice in my heart saying, "Sherri, when he falls head over heels in love with Me, he can't help but treat you right."

When Jimmie got home and realized what had happened, he was so kind. From that time on he began to communicate and build trust in every way. He worked at becoming a man, a husband and father and he kept his word.

At that time I learned how to put a period on our past and not go back there anymore. Because the past is just that, the past. And we can't change it; we can only start in the present to rewrite our future. When someone is trying to change, we need to forgive and forget the past. The key is this: If we are trying and taking steps to change, we take ownership of what we ourselves need to change. Because the only person we can actually change—with the help of the Holy Spirit and the Word of God—is ourselves. We won't do everything right all the time, but as long as we are willing, God will meet us there and help us.

> "As long as we are willing, God will meet us there and help us."

One day this thought entered my mind, "You've never finished anything." I had never thought about my life like that before. Nevertheless, the statement was true. I'd never finished anything. I quit school days after I turned sixteen, I couldn't keep a job, I never finished anything…ever. What was so shocking to me about this moment was for the first time, I had something that I really wanted to finish. I wanted to be a success in life, but the overwhelming thought in my mind was, *Will I quit on Jesus?* What I felt in that moment was that it would just be a matter of time before I threw my hands in the air and walked away from all that God had started in my life.

One day during my commute home from work it hit me, I have the DNA of a quitter and there's nothing I can do about it. I had to face the fact that the only thing I was successful at was quitting. In that moment I was scared, I mean I was freaking out. I knew I was destined to fail.

> "Father, I don't want to quit on what you've started in me. I want to finish what you've started in my life. Help me to finish."

Then suddenly I heard these words coming out of my mouth, "Father, I don't want to quit on what you've started in me. I want to finish what you've started in my life. Help me to finish." Well, I can't claim that I've made it. I can only say that still to this day, I pray that prayer. "Father, help me to finish."

I didn't know it at the time, but part of being

born again is the promise of a new nature. I like to think of it as a new DNA. After all, when you're born you receive the genetics of your parents by default. So it makes sense that when we are born again, we receive the genetics of our Heavenly Father. So being born again I was born into a new family, with new DNA, and I was no longer trapped in the habits of my past, like quitting.

I'm sure you are just like me and you want to succeed, you want to win, you want to finish. We all do. It is part of our nature, part of the image of God that we are created in. But just like the first family Adam and Eve, we all need help, and that help is always available to us if we will just ask. Simply ask God for the help that you need to finish. Pray this prayer with me right now. "Father, I come to You and I am asking for Your help. I am asking for You to permeate my life, come into my heart, forgive me and help me. I want to know Your love; I want to know Jesus. I want a new beginning. Amen."

CHAPTER ELEVEN

Confronting the Chaos

Even though our experience with God was real and even though we had been born again, we still had to change our thinking and our actions. We had programmed ourselves with triggers and responses. You know, if I would say something hurtful, it would trigger something from our past and BAM, we would be fighting again. Our home was a chaotic mess and we were the ones that were making it that way. At some point we had to step back and admit the truth:

The chaos was of our own creation. Our home had become the battleground and the war was raging.

There was a war in progress and it was being waged in our living room. What was the war about? It was about control. That is what every war is about and ours was no different. We were fighting with our emotions, and whoever shouted the loudest, pouted the longest, or even whoever was silent the longest would win. So the chaos continued; but every now and then the smoke would clear, and the sun would peer through, and we would get a glimpse of what it could be like. Even more than seeing it, we could feel what it could be like. I soon became hooked on that feeling. What was it? It was the feeling of peace. As I mentioned earlier, I was and still am a "peace freak." Once I sensed that feeling, I was on a quest. How do I get that to be in our home all the time? How can that be the norm and not the exception?

I was constantly looking for mentors. Men who could help me be a man, husband and father, and one of those men was a guy named J. Harold Lee, or Brother Lee, as we called him back then. Brother Lee was a Methodist pastor from Selma, Alabama. He was a tall, thin, witty man, and his eyes seemed to look right through me. But in his eyes was a deep love for Jesus, and it was so infectious. He was part of our struggle almost from the beginning. During the time we were divorced, Sherri attended church with my sister Patsy, Brother and Sister Lee and their kids. Because we fought so much, Sherri and I agreed that it was best if we not see each other at all. So she would bring Jason to the church, drop him off, and leave. Then I would come and pick him up. It was a crazy, chaotic mess, but for that time it worked and that's all that mattered.

One day I called the church and Brother Lee answered the phone. He made an attempt to minister to me, and I went off like a cannon. Boom! Cuss word after cuss word I let him have it. I can't believe I was that angry at anyone—especially this kind, Southern gentleman—but I was. Maybe it's because he was in my way, messing with my control. A few months after we were remarried we were having breakfast with Brother Lee and he mentioned my explosion. I had no idea he was the man on the other end of phone that day. His kindness and genuine love for us both was the only emotion I felt. I felt so bad for cussing this kind, Southern gentleman out.

In his mid-thirties, Brother Lee suffered a debilitating stroke that left him paralyzed on one side of his body. Life was not easy for the Lee family from that point on. About the time we met the Lees, three of their four kids were still living at home. Two teenage boys, Jimmie and John Ed, and one small surprise that arrived later in life, a baby girl Karen. When we would visit the Lee's home I would sense something. Really, I would feel something. It was something that I craved, something I longed to feel in our home…it was peace.

I remember leaving the Lee's house one night

and thinking to myself, "I want my home to be like theirs; full of peace." One thing I remember about their boys was how polite they were. We are talking teenage boys being polite! How does that happen?

> "I want my home to be like theirs; full of peace."

One Sunday evening Brother Lee was speaking at The Sheep Shed and he said something that rocked my world. "There are two things in life that I cannot do. Two things that I have to ask God to help me with every day." Now when he said that, he had my undivided attention. This guy was a rock star to me. I thought this man could do anything. My heart was open and I was listening for what he said next, "Two things I don't have the power to do, be a husband and father. I have to ask God for the help of the Holy Spirit every day for the wisdom and power I need to be a husband and a father." When he said those words of faith, they exploded in my heart. You mean I don't have to do this alone? You mean I can ask God for help and He will help me? I had never heard anything more wonderful in my life than those words that revealed to me God would help me be a man, be a husband and be a father. I didn't know what that meant, but I knew I wanted it and I wanted it bad.

Jesus told His followers that He would send the Holy Spirit—or as He called Him, "The Helper"—to each of us. This truth had suddenly come alive in me. I could ask God for help and He would help me. So that is what I did. I would ask God, "Help me to be the man, husband, father that You know I can be." It's a prayer that I pray to this day, and it is one that I know God loves to answer. The book of James says it like this, *"If any of you lacks wisdom, you should ask God, who gives generously to all without finding fault, and it will be given to you."* James 1:5 (NIV) How exciting is that? He doesn't look at our "faults," He doesn't look at what we lack or even at what we have. He just begins to dump wisdom—"help"—on us. Why? Because He is our Father.

When we look at the working of the Holy Spirit in the life of the believer, it is amazing. The Bible tells us that the result of this relationship with the Holy Spirit will produce the following things in our lives: *"But the fruit of the Spirit is love, joy, peace, forbearance, kindness, goodness, faithfulness, gentleness and self-control. Against such things there is no law."* Galatians 5:22-23 (NIV); meaning that these things will simply start showing up in my life as I "allow" them to. Or, let me say it like this: They will start showing up in my life as I give up my control.

Destruction and chaos are replaced with other emotions and other actions. Powerful emotions and actions that produce a life worth living. The kind of emotions that everyone of us want to have in our homes and families. As I started asking for help, these results started showing up in my heart and appearing in my life. I started responding differently to Sherri.

I found new ways to talk to her without tearing her apart. The smoke began to clear from the battlefield and I could see our home—our future—clearly for the first time. It didn't happen overnight. It happened step-by-step as I would surrender my desire to control everything. Piece-by-piece the puzzle started to come together.

As we each yielded to the help of the Holy Spirit in our lives, we started finding new ways of doing things. For instance, one evening coming home from work, I pulled in the driveway facing our house, shut the car off and just sat there. I didn't want to go inside because I knew there was the possibility that an angry woman was in there. Angry, more than likely, because of something stupid that I had said or done. But nevertheless I was just tired of failing, tired of the chaos, weary from the battle. So I sat there in my beat up old car waiting for something. For what? I didn't have a clue. I was just ready for a change.

It seemed like I sat there forever, but I am sure

it was only a few minutes. Then it happened. Help from the Holy Spirit exploded in my heart. I didn't know what it was at the time. In that moment it felt like I was just frustrated, but these words began to come out of my mouth as I pointed my finger at my house and shouted, "The peace of God lives in that house and those people who live in that house are people that are ruled by the peace of God. That house has a testimony of the peace it possesses." I had no idea what I was doing at the time, but some how, some way I found this strange peace in the words that I had spoken. Something was changing and it began in that moment. I found wisdom from God, help from the Holy Spirit, and inside, I knew things were different.

Now I know what was happening. What happened is I had asked for help from the Holy Spirit and He helped me. The words that I spoke weren't just plain old words. When I spoke those words I was prophesying to my life. I was speaking the words of God, the promises of God, into my world.

I was speaking about the future of my home and family. Those words carried some serious power with them.

As I began to yield my heart to those words and continued to speak them, things changed. There was a change in the environment/atmosphere of our house. Where there was once chaos, now we found peace. Where there was once turmoil, now there was calm. That didn't mean we didn't still fight, because we did. What it did mean was that we began to see a different future for us. It was the future God saw, the future God planned for us. It was a future of peace and not war, of staying married and not another divorce.

We became addicted to this peace. We craved it and anytime we violated it, we knew it, and would quickly deal with whatever we had done, and do whatever it took to return to that place of peace. It wasn't long before that prophecy was fulfilled and our friends and family would comment about the peace in our home. Really, even to this day, people who come to our house will say something like this, "It is just so peaceful here." Sherri and I know exactly what they mean, and we know exactly how and when it began.

Just a mouthful of frustrated words empowered by the help of the Holy Spirit with the power to create, created peace in our lives.

Words are so powerful; your words create your world. The proof is you have the spouse, the house, the kids, the job, etc., because of something that you said. Words can be constructive or destructive! What do you want to create in your house, spouse, kids, work and everywhere you are? Jimmie and I had used destructive words throughout our relationship, and it didn't create what we desired in our lives. We wanted love, joy, peace, and safety, but in order to have that we needed to understand the power of our words.

Jimmie and I knew how to use our words against each other, and we were great at it! The truth is, we wanted to be different, but we were ignorant! There is a story that comes to mind about myself. One night we had company for dinner and I began to cut Jimmie down right in front of our friends. Then I heard a very strong voice in my heart saying:

"Sherri, do I live in you?" And I responded in my heart with a yes! Then He asked, "Do I live in Jimmie?" And I said, yes! Then He asked, "Is that how you would talk to Me?"

Well, you know the answer to that! Of course not! I had been convinced by the Holy Spirit to find a better way. The Bible is very clear to teach us about our words, the power of the tongue, and what we create. I can't say I did it perfectly every time from then on, but I kept working on it.

In Proverbs 18:21, it says, *"Death and Life are in the power of the tongue and they who indulge in it will eat the fruit of it whether unto death or unto life."* Funny how the next verse, 22, says: *"He who finds a (true) wife finds a good thing and obtains favor from the Lord!"* (AMP)

And more than anything, I wanted to be a true wife.

In another translation it says it this way: *"Death and Life are in the power of the tongue, and those who love it and indulge in it will eat its fruit and bear the consequences of their words. The man who finds a wife finds a treasure, and he receives favor from the Lord."* Proverbs 18: 21-22 (NLT)

CHAPTER 12

We Grew Up Together - Kids Raising Kids

In August of 1977, another wonderful blessing arrived, Amanda was born! She had my heart from the moment I saw her. She is the baby of the crew and what a personality. She was the strong willed child of the bunch, but that never overshadowed her real personality. She was always singing, dancing, skipping through the house and laughing. When you are around Amanda, there's going to be laughter.

Sherri had chosen her name and when she first told me she wanted to name her Amanda I said, "No way." There was a song on the radio at the time called "Mandy" by Barry Manilow, and I hated it. I wouldn't allow one of my kids to be tormented their entire life by that song. Then one day I heard another song by Don Williams titled "Amanda." The chorus goes:

Amanda, light of my life, they should have made you a gentleman's wife.

I said, "Her name will be Amanda." I think I gave Amanda a million nicknames. She was Bud, Manders, but the one that stuck was "Pooh." One of our close friends' daughter, Becki, was a few months older than Amanda. I think she was about two and she tried to say Amanda's name one night and it came out like this, Amanda, Panda, Panda, Panda, Pooh. So it stuck.

Amanda

I will never forget how I felt with the birth of both of my kids. With Jason, in so many ways, I wished it could have been better for him. But looking back now, God gave us all a new beginning and a fresh start. Then when Amanda was born, we weren't perfect either, but we had met Jesus and we were changing our way of living. I remember thinking of the contrast between where we were emotionally when each of them was born. Jason had the love of Jimmie, his mom and dad, and my dad also loved him so. When Amanda was born, my due date was on my dad's birthday, August 9th. He was so excited to think they would have the same birthday, but she came a day early and he was okay with that. Jimmie was so elated with being in a different state of mind when Amanda was born and so happy that we could all enjoy a new beginning together.

We truly did grow up together, in many ways. Our kids both have been so kind, loving, and caring and they bring such joy in our lives. They gave up their beds lots of times to visiting strangers, and loved people so generously. I would have to watch Amanda because if she had a friend say they liked something of hers, well, it would go home with them. I love them both to pieces.

Jason & Amanda

Just a few weeks after Amanda arrived we "loaded up the truck" and moved to Caldwell County, Missouri. First, to be near The Sheep Shed and our new church family; and second, to get away from our old lives and old friends. Caldwell County at that time was one the smallest counties in the state. Man! This is country living for sure, talk about Green Acres! If you needed anything from the store you had to get it before 5:30 p.m. because that's when everything closed in town. We found a farm house five miles back on a gravel road and we moved in. We were 23 years old, with two kids, living back in the woods, and oh yeah, the house had no heat.

First Family Picture

We didn't know anything about raising kids, shoot we were kids ourselves. We just knew enough to know that God would help us. Today, now that the kids are grown and the grandkids have arrived, I can look back and see how we were successful and where we failed. Let me define success: As a family today we still love each other, we still laugh a lot when we are together and we are committed to doing life together to the end. So allow us to share some of the things we've learned and some of the mistakes we've made.

It Doesn't Matter What You Don't Have

It took several years before I developed a consistent work ethic, so most of the time we just barely made it through. And if it weren't for our folks helping us, we would have never made it. There were times when we didn't have food, and yet somehow we never went hungry. It was always so supernatural. The point I am trying to make is that no matter what you have or don't have, that shouldn't keep you from doing life, being happy, and most of all, being a family. Yes, you must be wise and do all that you can to prepare for life, but that is not a substitute for living life right now—right here in the present. I think we become trapped by our own sense of lack and never experience life because we are always waiting for life to happen sometime in the future.

Many young couples have the goal of achieving

financial stability before starting their relationships. I have to tell you, to me, it doesn't make sense. I mean, what is the point? If you've found "the one" then why not get started building your lives together? It's the old "make it up as you go" model. You will never have all the answers before you start something. You will never get all your ducks in a row before you begin. So don't let fear of making a mistake stop you from experiencing the life, the person, the relationship you are destined to experience.

Yes, I understand that you have to use wisdom in making every decision. So by all means, ask God for wisdom, and be wise. But don't *not* make a decision because you are afraid. That is the worst mistake you can make because of the torment fear brings us.

For us, we didn't have a choice in the matter. We didn't have anything and it would be decades before we did. And you know what? Looking back, none of it mattered. What mattered most is that we were together (broke or not) doing life with our family.

Yes, as a man, husband and father it's hard not to live in regret, thinking I could have done a better. Regret is a monster that is never satisfied. I always desire better for my family, but at some point we have to stop looking at what we don't have or what we didn't do and be content with what we do have. The Bible tells us this: *"But godliness with contentment is great gain."* 1Timothy 6:6 (NIV) This verse tells us that "godliness," which is our faith in Jesus, joined with our "contentment" is "great gain." The word contentment in this verse means "a perfect condition of life in which no aid or support is needed." This speaks to us saying that contentment brings us to this place, spiritually and emotionally, where we realize that we have all that we need. This allows us to enjoy what we have, instead of looking for something else. So be content with what you have. You will find it's one of the greatest accelerants on planet earth.

Consistency

With the kids, one of the first things we learned was to be consistent. So many times we make things way too complicated, and with raising kids we have to keep it simple. Someone taught us early on that we needed to be consistent with our kids. When we told them "no" about something once, it was no from then on. It wasn't no today and yes tomorrow. In doing this we create consistent boundaries for our kids. Sherri and I first had to agree on these issues and this created a level of trust between us and with the kids. Don't confuse kids by being inconsistent.

We Did Everything Together

I am, and always have been, a super tech guy. I don't know, but there is just something about how I am made up that craves technology. I have, through the years, had this insight to know where the difference is between the bleeding edge and the leading edge. And yes, I learned that the hard way. So this tech craving I have and being from the old school is an advantage. I can see the benefits in both worlds. I see, understand and value the hyper-pseudo connectedness of our present culture and its benefits, and I have experienced first-hand (the old school) what it is like to function in a world without much technology. Both have advantages, but one will not replace the other.

For us as a family, by default (meaning we had no choice) we did everything together. It was back in the old school days and we had no choice. Yes,

Sherri and I had to go to work and the kids had to go to school, but when it came to our free time we did it together. Looking back, I think these were the moments that had the most lasting impact on our family, and it is what's made our family last. Now I'm not talking about creating co-dependent relationships where the kids cannot function without being controlled by the parents. I'm simply talking about

Jimmie, Sherri, Jason & Amanda 1983

doing things together.

By allowing our children to just "be with us," we taught them how to live life. I know it's simplistic, but it is the truth, and oh so powerful. They learned to respond to life by watching how we responded to life. We all can do the same with our kids, providing that we are people of character and living life in a way that is reflective of our family, The Family of God.

What I would encourage families to do is create moments when the tech is off. I know that's a miracle, but it is possible. And just do some things together. Again, create these natural moments that cause you to do things together as a family. Especially while the kids are growing up. You won't have those days forever, so grab them while you can.

I had this little two-man plastic bass boat. It was small enough that I could put it in the back of my pickup, and Jason and I would go fishing. Now, I didn't have some great mapped-out plan other than we hoped to catch some fish for dinner. When you ask Jason today about his childhood, these moments always come up.

With Amanda, I would be going someplace and just throw her in the truck and off we would go. She was, and still is my buddy. Nothing fancy, no tech required, just a dad with his little girl. Then there were loads of times when we would be volunteering and the kids would be with us. I can't tell you how important these times were for us as a family. They just look like every day, mundane, normal moments, but these are the things that life is made of. They will never be perfect, but in the long run, they will always speak so clearly and loudly. Make them, plan them, live them. You will be happy that you did. Here is how the Bible describes it: *So here's what I want you to do, God helping you: Take your everyday, ordinary life—your sleeping, eating, going-to-work, and walking-around life—and place it before God as an offering. Embracing what God does for you is the best thing you can do for him.*

Romans 12:1 (MSG)

Have Fun

When I speak about the monster of regret, I speak from a deep place within my heart. Regret is a subtle but very powerful emotion that can consume your life, if you allow it to. Regret is a cruel taskmaster that you must keep in control, keep it in its place. Yes, we all want to do better, and reflecting on the past is one way to learn. But, it can't be ongoing, there has to be a limit when the past is the past. One thing I learned from Jessica (you will meet her in an upcoming chapter), *"We can't change the past."*

So with that in mind, if there was one thing I would do differently with my kids, I would have had more fun. Once you get to know me, you will know that I am pretty much an all-or-nothing kind of guy. Then coming from a past where I craved discipline, you guessed it, I over corrected. I was very strict with my kids and if I regret anything about raising them, it would be that I was too consumed with them doing everything right. My desire for them to do things right was mainly based on my own ego more than anything else.

I allowed religious rules to dictate so many of my decisions instead of making decisions that were in the best interest of my family. Let me explain. I am all for having a solid committed church life. But church isn't all there is in life and if it becomes that, you are destined to be a very unhappy person. That is exactly what happen to me. I would base most of my decision making on what would the church (the people, the pastors) think of me if I did this, instead of making decision based on whether or not this the best decision for me and my family. Yes, put Jesus first, but that doesn't mean that your family is second. It's not either/or; it's either/and.

For example, I love baseball and I was a great baseball player, so it was automatic that Jason loved baseball and he, too, was a great player. When Jason got old enough to play ball he wanted to join a league, but practices and games meant that we would have to miss church. So I made the dumb decision to allow him to play ball but I would never be able to attend.

I would drop Jason off at the ball field and head to church. Leaving him alone, never celebrating his strikes, hits and wins. It's decisions like that I regret. Today we celebrate every victory as if it's the super bowl and I never regret celebrating those. So have fun, make fun, be a fun family.

CHAPTER THIRTEEN

Work Before Family Ministry Before Family

My ministry career started just a few days after coming to Jesus. Wood was the source of heat for The Sheep Shed and I wanted to help keep the people warm. So on a cold, snowy December morning we took to the woods. I told one of the farmers leading the group when I arrived, "I'm ready to work, where's a chainsaw?" He replied, "Son, you're just coming off drugs so you don't get a chainsaw!" Needless to say, he was right. He said, "See that pile of brush? Move it over here." So, I spent the day dragging brush from one pile to the other, but I was working for the Lord.

That would be just one of many, many days that we volunteered our time and talents to help the church, and we loved it. We looked forward to doing whatever was needed, and it didn't matter what it was; we just had this attitude that said, "I am willing, show me what needs to be done and I will try to do it."

But, I must tell you I had no work ethic. Sure I had worked jobs before, but not with any consistency. I would work till the newness was gone and I would quit and look for something more exciting. Working with the men of the church taught me how to work. I didn't know anything about keeping my word, showing up on time, giving my best effort and just doing a hard day's work.

People have asked me, "When were you called into ministry?" Some people have these "burning bush" experiences, some people hear a voice and others have all kinds of wild stories, but not me. For me it was like this: When I came to Jesus and got up from that altar, I just wanted to do something for Jesus. He had done so much for me and I simply wanted to give back, so we started.

This was, and is, a family affair with us. Whenever we worked at the church we just loaded the kids up and all of us would work. So this very quickly became part of our family time. In the early days it was so wonderful and very time consuming. Actually, it became all-consuming, which is part of my crazy personality. As I said, I'm an all-or-nothing type guy. Well, the same was true with volunteering at the church. It wasn't long before all of our free time was spent at the church.

Maybe it was just part of God's calling or maybe I needed some boundaries that I didn't have. I would say it was a little of both. But, we began planning everything in our lives around church. This soon started to damage my family. They began to feel like they were second in everything and never the priority. It took many years before I would realize and correct this in our home. So don't fall into this trap.

With everything there must be boundaries. That was something we knew nothing about. So like Jimmie said earlier, we were all in with no limits.

I helped clean the church, yes, even cleaned the toilets with Jimmie. I taught in the Christian school for 12 years as a full-time volunteer; we helped with the nursery; Jimmie played on the worship team; and we always had people in our home. The thing was, we did life with our church family and every time there was something to be done, a service, a class being taught or a meeting, etc., we were there. Yes, it became all consuming and we didn't realize or notice the dreams of our kids.

What started out to be a very innocent, earnest desire, soon became more than we could handle. You see, knowing and following Jesus is about family. It is all about personally experiencing a loving relationship with a perfect Father, and a brother, Jesus, who was willing to give His all so you and I could experience this wonderful family. Anything that takes away from that will evolve into dead works. Meaning, good things that can produce no real life.

We stayed at The Sheep Shed from 1976 till 1993. What started out to be so pure, over time, became so toxic. What started out for me as just following Jesus, soon became all about pleasing man instead of God. What a trap that was for me and my family. Eventually, it became very apparent that our time at The Sheep Shed was over. I then lead my family to a place that was so different but soon we would find ourselves trapped in performance instead of relationship again.

I took an associate pastor position at one of the fastest growing churches in America. The church was very successful and very demanding and soon I found myself back in the same trap I had just left. With my eyes on man more that God, I fell right back into the same religious trap, performance before relationship.

After five years of very successful ministry I was toast and the only thing I could do was cry out to God for help. I had lost my passion for Jesus and needed help finding it again. One day I heard

(This page was left out of print and has been added)

in my heart, I heard this question, "Can you do this for the rest of your life?" My answer was yes. After all we were very successful so, yes. Then the question continued. "Can you do this for the rest of your life and be happy?" I knew as soon as I heard those words what my answer would be. No. So Sherri and I started to dismantle our lives.

On March 1, 2000, we resigned our very successful positions and had no idea what would happen next. From then till now we have done our best to stay connected to Jesus. We have not allowed ourselves to again be trapped performing for men rather than knowing, walking and experiencing the love of God for ourselves. After all, what The Father desires from us is our trust, which is really all that faith is about. Do we believe that God is worthy of our trust? That is the real question. The most intimate part of that is trust and trusting God with yourself.

Jimmie the Preacher

CHAPTER FOURTEEN

Our Kiss from Heaven

Every now and then God will seemingly, from out of nowhere, do something that leaves you speechless. I mean your mouth is hanging open (I call it frog-facing), you're in shock. It's so wonderful there are no words to describe it. Sherri called this moment in our lives "Our Kiss from Heaven."

Our Father is a redeemer. I think it is one of the most interesting parts of His character. At the core of His nature (I would call it "emotion") is this:

He is actively seeking to redeem all that is His—all of His family, all of His sons and daughters, all the whosoevers that will come to Him. He can't help Himself from going into full-on seek and redeem mode. It is so wonderful to experience. It's like He is just showing off. Like He says, "Stand back and watch this," and WHAM it's a full-on MMA match. Only instead of beatings, loving is on the card. Well, something wonderful like this happened to our family. Let me tell you about our "Kiss from Heaven."

As you have read about our pasts, we haven't tried to hide anything. We have laid it all out there for the world to see, and our hope is that it will help someone. Let me just say that writing some of this book was very, very hard to do. Why? Because we had to relive all of those old hurts and emotions that we walked away from so many years ago. But sometimes in the hurt and pain of the past, God will put His finger on something and say, "I'm going to redeem that!"

I thought that I qualified for the blessings of God on my life from December 19, 1976, forward. In my religious mind that meant that anything good that happened in my life from that day forward was God's blessing. Till one day, out of nowhere, God reached back in time, back into my past to a time when I didn't know or serve Him, and put His hand on part of my life and said. "I'm going to redeem this. So get out of My way."

Before I meet Sherri, as you've read, I was a really a mess. Out of control, undisciplined, selfish…a horrible kid. My world revolved around me and I thought I was in control, but really I was just out of control and wild. You've read all that already, so I'll go on.

When I was seventeen I was dating a girl off and on. I use the word dating loosely…mainly we were partying and at the end of the night we would end up in the same bed together. One fall evening I heard the words, "I'm pregnant."

"What?"

"I'm pregnant."

So in typical Jimmie mode, I hid. Months passed and I heard that she had a little girl. Months turned into years, years turned into decades until thirty-eight years later the silence was broken.

On February 13, 2011, I receive an email from the girl I dated nearly four decades ago. I opened it and read these words. "It's overdue that you should meet your daughter and your grandsons. Her name is Jessica, you can look her up on Facebook. She doesn't know about you yet." I responded immediately, "Just tell me when and where and I will be there." I am so grateful that after all these years, she had the courage to reach out to me.

Then it hit me like a brick to the head. How could I do this to one of my children? I mean really? I would never intentionally, purposely hurt one of my children, but I had completely abandoned Jessica. Grief hit my heart like a truck and the only prayer I could pray was really nothing more than a groan. I would groan out my prayer before God day and night. I would say, "Oh God, Jessica."

For the next three weeks Jessica was silent and as grief hit me, fear hit her. "Who is this man? What does he want? And why now?" Then on March 8th I got an email from Jessica and we started on a what may well be the wildest ride of redemption that we could have ever experienced. How could all of our past, all of this hurt, all of the rejection be redeemed? Well, let me just say, God started showing off as both of our families opened up our hearts and said to God, "We are willing, let's see what You can do."

What happened next was wild. As we started walking through discovery after discovery, step by step, finding the redeeming, forgiving, ever powerful, love of the Father, we found this beautiful, kind, wonderful girl who is my daughter Jessica, and her husband LeRoy, and their four sons, Mat, Seth, Aaron and Jacob.

Not being bound by time, He reached out His hand, went back into my past and said, "I'm going to redeem this." There is so much more to the story that we would love to share with you but we are going to save that for a book that we are in the process of writing. Let me just tell you this one story that really describes how our family is today:

Jason, Jessica & Amanda

Easter Sunday 2011, was our first church service together. Sherri and I were at Jessica and LeRoy's house getting ready for church. I was drinking a cup of coffee when Jessica appeared with a gift for me. It was a coffee mug with "Daddy" written on it, full of her favorite candy bar, Zero Candy Bars. She had no way of knowing those are my favorite candy bars, too. As we were talking, she reached up and touched my face and said, "Daddy it's just like you were always here!" WOW! That is exactly what our relationship is like. There is no void, there is only a family fully restored by the power of God. A Big Kiss from Heaven!

Walking through this time I was reminded of this verse, "*Now to Him who is able to do exceedingly abundantly above all that we ask or think, according to the power that works in us...*" Ephesians 3:20 (NKJV). God is at work in your life. Don't limit His working to your own words or mind. Because He is in the mind-blowing business.

CHAPTER FIFTEEN

Where Are We Now?

On writing this book it has been forty years since we stumbled into God's Sheep Shed, and what a life we have lived. Neither Sherri nor I planned on living this long, but we are so glad that we did. The past forty years hasn't been easy, but it has been remarkable; and looking back we can agree with that scripture that says, *"Now to Him who is able to do exceedingly abundantly above all that we ask or think, according to the power that works in us…"* Ephesians 3:20 It's been beyond anything that we could have dreamed up. Today it is something that is so remarkable, so wonderful that it defies words.

Since 2000, and until the present, Sherri and I minister in churches weekly throughout the United States and some in the United Kingdom. My music creates the opportunity for us to be in all manner of non-church venues like bars, clubs, music festivals, motorcycle rallies and prisons. We have a deep love for people everywhere we go and we have found no one that Jesus doesn't love.

Jason lives in Dallas, and works as a chef. He continues to write music and is an active blogger. He has a mind for ministry, business, and is a friend's friend. If you make Jason your friend, he will be there till the end. I co-wrote one of my most requested songs "Jupiter & Mars" with Jason. He has a gift with words that comes down from generations of our family.

Amanda, lives in a small town just outside of Kansas City. She works with us here in the ministry.

Amanda has a passion for the things of God and a voice that you must hear. Check out my "LIVE on the 4th of July" DVD and you will see Amanda singing in the background. She is married to Chris and they have five children, Jake, Kelly, Brianna, Mikaela and Zayne. When you're around Amanda she will be laughing.

Jessica lives near Washington, DC, where she and LeRoy work for The Defense Department. Jessica has a passion for ministry and life like few people I have met. Jessica and LeRoy have four boys, Mat, Seth, Aaron and Jacob.

Even though we are spread out across the country, we are still a very close family. We talk or text many times a week, and we get together as much as we possibly can. When we are together you can expect music to be playing, we will be constantly picking on each other, we will be loud and laughing. There will also be BBQ cooking and there will be large quantities of love.

The Family

And that, my friends, is how you go from Granny paying for your divorce to having a wonderful life, with God's help, one day at a time, one step at a time, and not leaving anybody behind. Jesus said it like this: "But Jesus looked at them and said to them, '*With men this is impossible, but with God all things are possible.*'" Matthew 19:26 (AKJV)

Peace,

Jimmie & Sherri

More Books by Gungor Publishing

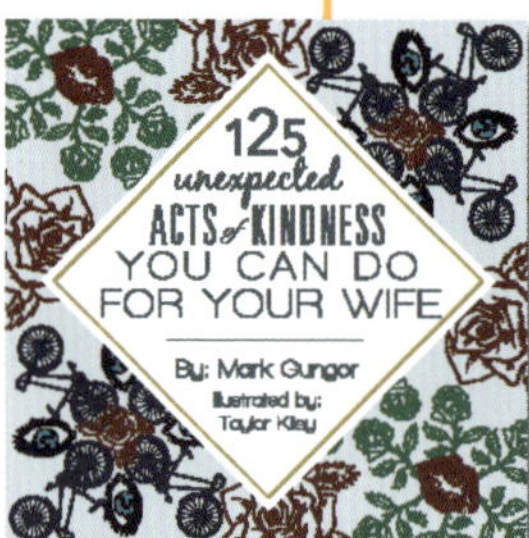

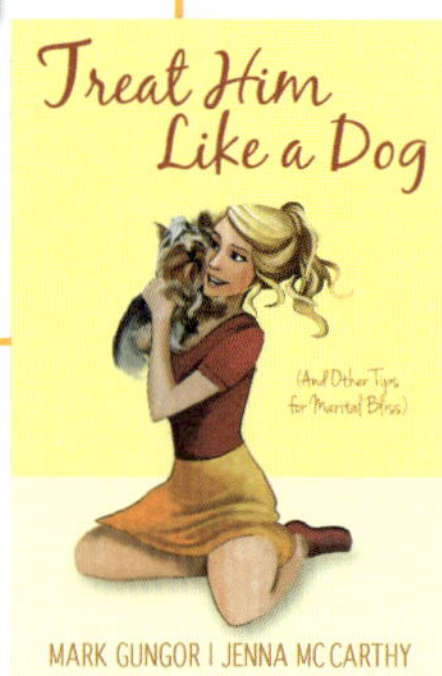

markgungor.com